MUXIE
MINDSET

MOXIE MINDSET

Secrets of Building a Profitable,
Independent Physicians
Practice in a Competitive Market

DINA D. STRACHAN, MD

purposely
created
PUBLISHING

MOXIE MINDSET
Published by Purposely Created Publishing Group™
Copyright © 2018 Dina Strachan

All rights reserved.

Printed in the United States of America
ISBN: 978-1-948400-61-9

Special discounts are available on bulk quantity purchases by book clubs, associations and special interest groups. For details email: sales@publishyourgift.com or call (888) 949-6228.

For information logon to:
www.PublishYourGift.com

DEFINITION OF MOXIE

1. ENERGY, PEP

    ▸ Woke up full of *moxie*

2. COURAGE, DETERMINATION

    ▸ It takes ... *moxie* to pull up roots and go to a land where the culture and probably the language are totally foreign

    —**M. J. McClary**

3. KNOW-HOW

    ▸ Was impressed with his musical *moxie* and hired him as a solo

Source: Merriam-Webster Dictionary

This book is dedicated to all the doctors who went into medicine to help people and who still have the moxie to expect to practice AND live a life that they love, feeling happy and free. Doctors with the goal to burn bright—not burnout! We are so worthy!

#moxiemd #moxiemindset #moxiemoves

"Being fabulous is not for the faint of heart."

—Dr. Dina

"I earn, receive, and accumulate large amounts of extra money in happy, pleasurable ways for the good of all concerned."

—Phil Laut

TABLE OF CONTENTS

PREFACE

Truth be told, I never wanted to build a private practice. Becoming a doctor was just one of many things I had considered doing since childhood. As my mother had been a physician, it wasn't exotic and mysterious to me. She was a psychiatrist at a state hospital and had, at times, been in private practice, but never seemed to be able to handle the business side well. When I finally decided to pursue a career in medicine, I was attracted to it, not because of what I had seen, but by the many options. As a doctor, I could have a role anywhere in the country—or the world. There were so many professional settings one could work in. There was clinical work in a hospital, community clinic, or a private practice. And in addition to clinical care there was research, public health, administration, academia, or even industry.

When I started my career in medicine, what I had envisioned was a sort of academic-artist lifestyle. My hard work and achievements would bestow on me the opportunity to be taken care of as an employee of a prestigious university hospital. I imagined that the university would shelter me from certain responsibilities. Although I could ostensibly make more money out in a community practice, I would do well and get to enjoy a stimulating professional environment protected from what I perceived as the boring, business aspects of healthcare. Instead, supported by my lofty institution, I would do beautiful things with my training like serve the underserved, work on interesting projects, travel and share my expertise with colleagues, inspired students and physician trainees. My service would be appreciated. It might feel like a respectful, sugar daddy type arrangement. Even if, allegedly, for a little more money, I could not imagine why someone would choose what I perceived as the mom-and-pop-shop-ball-and-chain lifestyle of private practice.

This illusion didn't last long. By the time I was finished with my training and setting out to start practice in the late 1990s, the medical industry, even academia, had changed. It had become more corporate, and doctors were starting to feel the economic impact of these changes. Practicing medicine had always been seen as a recession proof business. We were trained by people who taught us, "just do good and the money will come." It was considered in bad taste for a doctor to be interested in how the healthcare dollar flowed. I was led to believe that because I had gone to great schools, Harvard and Yale, and had trained at a great place, the University of California, San Francisco, in the sought-after specialty of dermatology, that I would be set. But by the time I was ready to start my career as a board certified dermatologist, it was beginning to look as if what had been true for those before us would not be true for the next generation of doctors.

I run a profitable, independent private practice in the most competitive market, New York City, in the most competitive specialty, dermatology, in the country. Having the option to practice independently is one of the corner stones of American medicine. Before I started, I never perceived that doing this would be hard, but perhaps uninteresting. I was wrong in both cases. Running a business has been far from boring. It has demanded that I grow in all areas of my life. Everyone in my life has benefited by me having my own business. But I had to change my mindset to make it happen. To build an independent medical practice among giant hospital networks, and venture capital funded mega groups, I had to tap into my New York Moxie, or #moxiemindset. Moxie is, essentially, energy, courage and know-how. I never imagined that starting a business would take so much energy—but it did. I was shocked at the amount of courage I needed to weather the difficulties—but I found it. Who knew the amount of know-how it would require to make it happen—but I found it.

This book is for doctors who are interested in venturing off into private practice—profitable and happy, private practice. It's also for doctors who may already be in practice and who are struggling with the process. Because we are doctors, we often feel we are failing when we struggle. To have made it to the point of having a medical degree, one may have accomplished things that seem impossible to other people. We are accomplished in medicine and we may have forgotten that that wasn't always so. When we take on tasks like starting a business, we may have forgotten that the uncertainty, the fear, and the struggle is just a sign of us choosing to grow beyond our comfort zone. We've been there before—and we survived. It's part of the process. The struggle is real.

Even if a person is smart and accomplished, like most doctors are, our training and mindset may set us up to fail in business. We think we should already know everything. We think we shouldn't look out for our interests. Some say that doctors aren't good at business. But doctors can learn business, too. They tell us doctors shouldn't care about the money. What they usually mean is that we shouldn't care about *our own* money—but about someone else's. And they tell us that doctors should be humble—lest they be accused of having a "God complex." This, all while an increasing number of people with less training, "play doctor" with real patients. While we are to worry about being perceived as arrogant, people with less expertise and without accountability to patients seize healthcare resources and leadership. Doctors are probably smarter than the average person. If they humble themselves like they did to earn the title "doctor," and learn what they have to learn, be it about marketing, or about themselves, they too can enjoy starting a profitable business, free of some of the demands of those with the intention to exploit. In this book I share some of the lessons I learned navigating this brave new world of medical care.

As with any success, we are always standing on someone's shoulders. As a latch-key-Generation-X child, I've always found comfort in figuring things out for myself. But no one does it alone. When I was ready to really explore the edges of my comfort zone, the coaches came. As a former athlete, I had associated coaching with sports, but whenever we set out to do anything challenging, be it playing sports, or starting a business, the people who succeed seem to always be open to continued guidance along the way. I wouldn't have a business, a life that I love, nor would I be writing a book about it, if it weren't for my first business coach, the late, great Phil Laut, author of *Money Is My Friend*. I always chuckle as I remember the sound of him casually chewing, what sounded like cereal, on our coaching calls, as he dropped pearls of knowledge about money that changed my life. Marketing master, Coach Fabienne Frederickson, taught me that even though I was a physician who went into medicine to "help everybody," that I, too, had the right to attract those whom I wanted to work with. I had never considered my own preferences before. But doctors, too, are human. They too have a right to choose with whom they work. I worked with spiritual business coach and author, Joe Nunziata, with whom the learning felt like therapy rather than business training. From him I learned that bumps in the road were often a sign of success, and that until I healed my own feelings and inner conflicts, even when it seemed I was doing everything right, that the same problems were going to show up in my business. In his words, "If the doctor ain't happy, ain't nobody happy." His wisdom helped me face "imposter syndrome" when I had trouble accepting that success doesn't always feel like one expects. It helped me carry on without burning out. Internationally recognized marketing geniuses, JT Foxx and Jason Gilbert, taught me to have the courage to shine and promote my fabulous brand. I am forever grateful to the amazing Dr. Drai (Dr. Draion Burch), Dean of The Medical Moguls Academy, who made me write this book (despite my kicking and screaming). Dr. Drai is uniquely talented in helping people uncover their gifts. He helped me see that I had been so busy with my hustle that I never realized I had built much of anything. Dr. Drai revealed to me that people were inspired by my moxie—and wanted me to help them find theirs. And I can't leave out my physical and spiritual coach, trainer, Terrell Stanback. With 50 squats and a prayer he helped maintain my fitness to do God's work, and reminded me that God was always winking in the background.

So if you are a doctor who wants to start a practice, or who already has a practice, and wants to make sure it's profitable while you feel good about your business and life, then keep reading. Think of this as a Tao for Doctors or like *The Art of War*, but for doctors on the front lines of private practice.

CHAPTER 1

....

Ride the Wave of Thoughts and Feelings

"There are no wrong notes in jazz. It's the note you play afterwards that makes it right or wrong."

—Miles Davis

I was living the life! Living near the beach in Los Angeles, with college, medical school, internship and residency behind me, I was finally starting to enjoy some of that gratification I had delayed. In my first job, which was a teaching position at a county hospital in South Central, I got the satisfaction of sharing my skills in a community that needed them. My main responsibility was to supervise dermatology residents. There were six. I got to teach and make sure excellent medical care was provided. I would get dual faculty appointments from Charles R. Drew University of Medicine and Science, which was across from the hospital, and from the prestigious University of California, Los Angeles. Although I took on a lot of responsibility fast in this position, it was a kind of dream job for me. I was doing good, lived in a fabulous city, and had independence, as well as reasonable hours with a reverse commute. Except occasionally on the weekends, I didn't understand why people complained about LA traffic. The County didn't pay as much as some places, but it had amazing benefits. Walking on the beach in my free time didn't cost much, nor did learning to surf and scuba dive less than a mile from my apartment—in February.

Don't hate me because I was happy. Some thought it was odd that I had accepted a position, somewhat "off the grid," at a small public hospital, after having attended world-class institutions. I was happy to leave San Francisco after finishing my training at the University of California. The city had not lived up to my expectations in terms of California sunshine or a cosmopolitan culture. But I never imagined myself in Los Angeles. Although I would have never admitted it, I had those stereotypes of superficiality and shallowness in my head. But, the residency of my dreams in San Francisco had been toxic. I had worked so hard to get exactly what I wanted, and found it disappointing. It was hard to get compassion, even from myself, because I was in a position that many envied. I was in dermatology at a prestigious institution in a popular city—but I was not happy there. My confidence was bruised because I had gotten my pick and felt like I had made the wrong decision. But, as is the nature of all things in the Universe, this wave of my career was about to break and another was coming. I would have to make some choices again—but I didn't trust myself. I was struggling in my thoughts and feelings.

One of the things I was most excited about when I moved to California was having the opportunity to learn to surf. The idea of being in flow with the forces of the earth seemed incredible, fun—but challenging. It was something that called to me, despite being from the East Coast and such a concrete jungle of a city. My strong aquatic skills as a competitive swimmer would help. I would soon learn, however, that catching a wave would require a perfect storm of confidence, know-how, effort and surrender—much like being a doctor or running a business. It takes a lot of effort just to get out past the break to even attempt to catch a wave. Then one has to turn around, study the surf and wait. When the perfect wave to ride is coming, it's time to paddle hard and pop up on both feet, just as the ocean lifts the board. To continue the ride, constant adjustments must be made to go with the flow. There is thinking involved, but one can't think too much. Surfing also requires the use of feelings.

I studied what my teacher said at the surf school, much like I had as a medical student. Then it was quickly off to the water. My lesson would continue until I had caught a wave. I wasn't sure if it was a good thing, but I caught the first wave I ever set out to ride. It was amazing but I didn't know what to do. I was surfing. On my first try I found what is called "the sweet spot." But in surfing, as in business, the location of a "sweet spot" shifts throughout the ride. Initially thrilled to be a New York girl riding a California wave as if it were the subway, I soon found myself about to collide with another surfer. I became aware and afraid in my inexperience. I started to think too much, came out of my feelings, and tumbled into the water. I didn't catch a wave the rest of that session. "Beginner's luck," I thought.

Doctors get into medical school because of their thinking, but what allows us to be successful with our patients, careers, and lives in the long-run requires us to also connect with our intuition and feelings—much like riding out a wave. I had a hard time thinking about what I wanted to do after residency because I didn't trust myself to choose, having had a bad experience. In my last year of training, when I was approached by the director of a program in Los Angeles, I mostly went to the interview as a courtesy. I was surprised, however, that Los Angeles felt good to me. I hadn't been accustomed to making decisions with my feelings. "What are you doing?" I thought to myself as I turned down other options. "This feels good, but isn't Los Angeles the land of illusion?" I was excited about my first job as a board certified dermatologist in this new city. Still, I cried myself to sleep on the floor of my Marina del Rey apartment my first night in Los Angeles. It turned out to be a good sign. It was my surrender to the wave. It was uncomfortable, but I had made a choice with my feelings. I'd eventually get used to expecting to feel good.

MOXIE MINDSET EXERCISE

We are in a time of an epidemic of "physician burnout." This is a complex issue. In part, the problem of burnout has to do with what we doctors think and feel about being a doctor. This influences the choices we make. A doctor who also runs a business has to get even more comfortable making decisions and choices. Being a happy doctor is a choice. Like riding a wave, it requires rolling with one's thoughts and feelings.

Write down your thoughts about the following:

1. What do you *think* about being a doctor? Do you *think* that doctors have a right to be happy? Do you *think* that doctors should be martyrs? Should they be perfect? Is it okay for them to also look out for their own interests—or just those of other people?

2. How do you *feel* about being a doctor? Does it *feel* good? Why or why not? Does it *feel* like it's what you are supposed to be doing? If no, what would make it so?

_____

_____

_____

_____

_____

_____

CHAPTER 2

·····································

Make Your Disadvantage Your Advantage

Although it was too early in my career for me to have the title "Residency Program Director," I was essentially running a residency program directly out of training, often on my own. My boss, a dermatology luminary, was frequently away on business, as he was my first day of work. I was not only in charge—I was it. "I guess he trusts me," I said to myself when I realized that, other than with the help of a senior resident and my boss's secretary, I had to learn the ropes on my own the first week. Much like many of the children of my generation, I was a latchkey...doctor. It's a good thing I had had some practice.

Having come from much bigger, competitive institutions that were resource rich, this was the first time in my medical career that there was a spirit of being the underdog. When I took the job, the program was on probation, mostly because there had been only one faculty member—my boss. With my arrival, that made only two. There was enough work, however, for many. Some people criticized me, as I was a double Ivy League graduate, for going on this path. Yes, it did hurt the ego a bit when I heard that some of my mentors were "worried" about my choice. But, it felt like the right thing to do at the time. And little did I imagine that my first academic job, in which I was dropped on the frontlines, would be the best training ground for becoming successful at doing what I thought I never wanted to do—run a private practice.

My frontline job was also good preparation for my board certification examination. Some people were able to take time off after training to focus only on studying. My boss needed me to start work shortly after I finished my residency, and with no trust fund in sight, I also needed to start working. Protected study time was not an option. It turns out I wouldn't need as much time to sit over a book reading about the exotic conditions I would be tested on, because I was actually managing such patients with these problems all day at the hospital. So in working, I studied for my specialty boards—and got paid.

As one has to do in a small business, I wore many hats as "Director of Resident Education." I was instantly a "boss," with both the authority and the responsibilities. In addition to teaching residents, I handled human resource matters, operations, compliance, and recruiting. I did some research projects. I also helped with coaching and mentoring. I started to understand why medical schools and residency programs looked for accomplishments and activities outside of those related to medicine. It's not just because well-rounded people are more interesting. Well-rounded people are necessary.

I was a less traditional medical school applicant; I majored in biology, but that was efficient. The required classes for my major also fulfilled the requirements to apply to medical school. I had never worked in a laboratory. I didn't want to. Instead, I did things that seemed relevant to medicine but more interesting to me than playing with test tubes. I took an elective, which entailed camping out in the Panamanian jungle, studying endangered monkeys and their environment. I ran film festivals. I took Spanish theater workshop classes. To the dismay of my family, I took time off after college to figure out what kind of life I wanted to have, still not certain that medicine was the path for me. This was considered flaky. And "taking time off" was somewhat audacious in my case. It was considered, at the time, a privilege reserved for people who, unlike me, had trust funds or indulgent sugar daddies. Undeterred, I created my own trust fund through a combination of jobs and cash fellowships set up by benefactors who liked to use their money to support young people doing interesting things. I backpacked through India and did a grassroots development internship, temped as a receptionist at a record company in New York, worked as a clinical research assistant on a breast cancer study, worked in catering parties and events, tutored wealthy children for the SAT, did transcription of pre-op medical examinations, and worked as a perinatal case manager in a community health center.

So, I had the experiences I wanted, and it turns out, it also made my resume look pretty impressive. Some of these experiences I sought out because they were interesting. Others, I pursued out of need. Both types gave me some advantages and skills, which allowed me to be resourceful and successful in my first "real" job. And this job, although it was academic, was much like running a business. At a bigger, richer institution, I would have been waiting years to have the opportunities I had in South Central Los Angeles. I got to practice my *business skills* before I had to pay those *business bills*—and before I knew I'd need them.

I stayed in that position at the county hospital for two years, and helped get the program off probation before I left. I cherish this experience, as it allowed me to learn the ropes of running something with little personal risk. These days, people seem to resent being employees. Instead, they aspire to step out and be the boss from the beginning. But sometimes, only when they've made the leap into running a business, do they realize some of the advantages of being an employee and learning on the job.

MOXIE MINDSET EXERCISE

A job is an opportunity that someone else creates, in which we can earn income and learn skills that we can use later. Even if you want to start your own business, or have one now, it's good to show gratitude. For example, many doctors remember residency as exploitative—but what about what we gained? Didn't other people share their expertise with us—essentially training the competition? Didn't we also get to learn how to treat patients who might have otherwise not let a novice come near them?

1. What skills and connections can you now use in business that you gained from being on a job? List them and give thanks!

2. Have you ever been in a position of seeming disadvantage that turned out to be an advantage? How did it all work out in your best interest?

_____

_____

_____

_____

_____

_____

CHAPTER 3

....

Get Up off the Nail–and Up on the Board

A man went to visit his neighbor, who was sitting on the front porch with his dog. The dog repeatedly whined. The man asked, "Why is your dog whining?" His neighbor responded, "Oh, he's just sitting on a nail." The dog whined again. Confused, the man asked, "Well why doesn't he just get up?" His neighbor calmly answered, "I guess it doesn't bother him enough."

—**Unknown**

Although I enjoyed my first job at the county hospital in Los Angeles, I did not see it as a long-term situation. The problem was that working in the county system felt limiting to me. Sure, I felt good every morning, no matter what drama I encountered at work, as I knew that I was providing a much-needed service to an underserved community, but the professional limitations of that system started to feel confining. Many of the people, including the doctors, were simply there for the stability and great benefits. It was just a job to some—which isn't necessarily a bad thing. To me, however, a job was somewhere I spent a lot of my time on earth. I wanted it to be something more than just a paycheck. I wanted to continue to grow—not just settle in. Something as simple as getting experience with medications that were not on the county formulary seemed out of reach. Although I had just started my career, I felt like I had hit the ceiling fast. I didn't even have a faculty practice to see patients on my own. I was always supervising a resident who was managing the patient. It was like intending to catch a wave but never standing up, riding belly down the whole time. I didn't want to lose my skills so I started to explore my options. I loved Los Angeles, and my life waking up to sunshine, the smell of the Pacific, and the sounds of people playing tennis. I wasn't, however, ready to retire. I was ready to grow. For me, that meant moving back home to New York.

When I first moved to California, I never imagined that I would want to move "back East," as they said out there, particularly to New York City, having experienced gentler places. But I was missing all those wonderful things that people come to New York for—the opportunities, the people, the excitement, as well as my friends and family. New York had so much to offer, but it could be a hard place to live—and it was an expensive place to live. Doctors were not at the top of the food chain in a city of bankers, real estate moguls, and trust fund kids. I was determined to go back, but I was coming back to live well, not struggle, in New York.

MOXIE MINDSET EXERCISE

1. Leaving a stable situation, even one we don't like, can take courage. What "nails" are you sitting on in your life and career right now? What will it take to make you get up off the nail? Doctors especially, can have issues with taking risks. What fears do/did you have with respect to venturing out on your own into practice? What fears do/did you have about staying where you were? How do you deal with these feelings?

CHAPTER 4

....

Training People How to Treat You Is the Way

Ironically, as I started job hunting, I noticed that "academic" positions were starting to look more and more like private practice jobs—unless one did basic science research. It wasn't enough to teach in a clinic, which has to generate money, or do research (which requires fund-raising), but academics also had to generate money in clinical practice, much like practitioners did in the community. Many of these jobs seemed to be just direct clinical work or practice. The difference was that in these large institutional settings, the doctor didn't have much influence on how things were done. The practices were often run by non-medical people, on high salaries, generated off of the work of the doctors, or entitled senior doctors who also had high base salaries and did not participate in insurance plans. They were not necessarily great at business, nor did they have to be, as they were not held accountable to the doctors whose work paid their salaries. The financial activity was not transparent. When I decided to take an academic job back in my home city of New York, a job that promised the mix of opportunities I had been looking for, I was in for a surprise.

First, I found that my good work ethic, instead of bringing rewards, was sometimes being used as a reason for someone to attempt to take advantage of me. For example, one of my colleagues, someone who had completed training at the same time I had, and at no more prestigious a place, had the audacity to invite me to work on clinical trials with him—unpaid. This is something that someone who had not already completed a training program might do—not someone who was already board certified and practicing. It was insulting. Further, living in New York was expensive. I hadn't gone into medicine just for money, but I still needed money to live and pay my own student loans.

Although I had moved to a more prestigious institution in New York, the environment didn't always feel so respectful. In addition, while I had expected to have time to build my own practice and work on developing my professional reputation and expertise, I found myself increasingly assigned to satellite clinics the hospital had acquired or had set up relationships with. Although there was a need in these settings, they were often unpleasant, poorly run places to work, where the doctors were not treated well. At the job I left in Los Angeles, also in an underserved area, the doctors had been treated with respect. At these satellite clinics for my new job, the administrators wanted even the contracted doctors, who did not get paid by-the-hour or get overtime, to punch a time clock. Working in these environments didn't seem like much of a career move, nor was it particularly lucrative. It was starting to feel like exploitation.

Perhaps one of the most disturbing assignments was being sent to cover a clinic in Harlem during my last year at the "academic" job. It wasn't the actual place that was of concern, but the reason my boss had decided to send me there. Somehow my position had turned into my having to run around Manhattan to six locations every week. I met with my boss a number of times to discuss that I wanted to consolidate my week and have my job look like what we discussed when I accepted the position. He promised to honor our agreement and pull me out of some of the satellite locations—until he assigned me to a seventh, additional, clinic instead.

This assignment took me by surprise, as he was pulling another colleague out of this clinic, a colleague who went to far fewer places than I did, in order to replace her with me. He had coverage for the site, so the decision didn't make sense to me. I was also concerned, because it further reduced my opportunities to develop my private faculty practice and bring in a bonus. When I discussed it with my chairman, he looked distressed and begged me to "trust" him. He said he really needed my help in this situation—but that he hadn't forgotten about our agreement.

Having come from a situation with an overburdened boss, I had empathy for all the responsibilities my new boss was juggling. I could tell there was something he was dealing with that he couldn't share with me. Trying to be a team player, and having compassion for the many stakeholders a department leader had to manage, I agreed to help him out, temporarily, and cover a seventh location for the department. I trusted him, although I didn't understand. It immediately became clear, however, that things were not going to work out at the new location on my first day.

I walked in and introduced myself to the woman sitting at the front desk. The facility was nice enough. It was clean and new. It had that basic, all-too-familiar, medical institution linoleum floor and the smell of disinfectant. Gentrification was already happening in Harlem, so there wasn't anything particularly menacing about the location. I was wondering what the issue with my colleague had been.

"I'm Dr. Strachan," I said. "The new dermatologist."

There was a pregnant pause before she asked me what I had already told her.

"YOU are the new dermatologist?" she asked.

"Yes," I said, again. I was a little annoyed. I thought they would have known I was coming. Hadn't they scheduled patients for me?

The woman smiled, but it wasn't friendly. Nor was her smile unfriendly toward me. It was the smile of someone who had just heard a juicy piece of gossip she wasn't supposed to know about.

She looked at me and started talking, but she wasn't talking to me. "This is the new dermatologist, y'all," motioning in my direction. "I guess the blond lady was scared!"

There were cackles of laughter coming from all around the clinic. I felt mocked. Not by the clinic staff—but by my boss and colleague.

I was furious. The receptionist was slyly letting me know that I was being used because of my race. She figured it out as soon as she saw me, as did everyone else who worked there. Because I was African American, I was being expected to do someone else's job because my colleague was uncomfortable working in Harlem. My boss had given her permission to drop her responsibilities and had assigned them to me. I was neither informed nor compensated for the favor. In fact, I was being financially punished for helping him.

Now my boss's distress when I asked him why he had assigned me to the Harlem clinic made sense. Now I understood why he would not explain this odd decision when I asked him why he was adding a site to my already over-extended schedule. Now I understood why he had asked me to "trust" him rather than telling me the truth.

What made it hurt more was that my boss was supposedly a champion of diversity in our field. He was also rumored to boast at national meetings about the credentials of the faculty in his department; some of the best credentials of which he bragged about were mine. He was using my credentials to boost his reputation, while disrespecting me and treating me as a pawn. It felt like exploitation—and my Ivy League pedigree was no protection. In fact, it might have been the cause. When I confronted my boss about the comment from the clinic staff, he neither admitted nor denied it. All I know is that I was out of that clinic in one month.

Yes, I stood up for myself, and this time, I got what I wanted. I knew, however, that I couldn't continue to work somewhere where the leader didn't respect my interests or care at all about my career. There were too many competing interests in this Machiavellian environment. It was a painful revelation, but it was reality. But this wasn't even the worst of it. With respect to the time I had been building my faculty practice, I soon discovered that I had been taken advantage of there as well.

MOXIE MINDSET EXERCISE

1. Doctors are often told not to worry about their own interests or stand up for themselves. Just do good work and you will be rewarded. This isn't always true. This way of thinking avoids dealing with the fact that we are being mistreated, because we don't want to do the work to address it or we are afraid of being judged. Have you been in a situation in which you were seen as valuable in terms of your contribution, but were treated more as a pawn than as a player? How did that feel? What did you do?

CHAPTER 5

··

Your Cut Doesn't Matter If They Don't Collect the Money

Part of my pay was based on incentive. This was important since moving back to New York meant that the cost of living was much higher than it was in California. As Manhattan was much more competitive, success was not certain—everyone had to hustle. This didn't scare me though. I was willing to hustle. But I also expected a return.

I was quickly building a following of patients. I was getting busy, but not seeing much bonus money, and wondered why. Again, it was difficult to find out what was going on with the money. I was told that insurance companies "just don't pay," and that I should think about having a cash only practice. But then I wondered why anyone would take insurance if the companies simply did not pay. I looked to the people who did billing to explain and give feedback. Had I used the wrong code? Was the service not covered? How could I do better? But it was like talking to a wall.

It turned out that the percentage of the money we collected was low. Although I had negotiated a good percentage, it was a high percentage of very little money. I also found that my practice was accepting patients whose insurances I hadn't been credentialed to accept. In those cases I wasn't being paid at all. When I asked why they would have me do work, and take on liability without the possibility of getting paid, they said that they had been too busy to follow up my credentialing applications, and that the hospital didn't want to lose patients. I didn't understand how the hospital could operate without collecting money for the work we did. Having us there, even if they didn't pay us, had a cost. It didn't make sense. The bottom line, however, was that the people in charge of operations somehow got their pay despite not collecting the fees, whether I got my bonus or not. They didn't work for me—and they didn't care.

When the hospital took on a new practice site that was already booked for weeks with appointments, I became more optimistic. It was a different location run by different people. The doctors were excited to inherit a busy office—a very unusual opportunity in Manhattan. I was quickly seeing a full schedule of patients, two sessions a week, and I looked forward to the first faculty meeting at which we were given the reports of how much money we had generated. Bonuses were paid out quarterly—so it was for three months of work.

I expected to see that thousands of dollars had been collected as a result of all of my hard work. I had seen many patients. The majority paid with insurance plans that reimbursed well. This is why I couldn't understand why the column on the report I was given at the meeting, the column which indicated how much money I had generated for the department, said I had only generated $10.

TEN DOLLARS.

And according to my boss, that wasn't a typo. As I looked at my report, I was confused. Just one patient copayment was generally more than $10. "Certainly," I thought to myself, "this is a mistake."

I interrupted the meeting.

"Excuse me, but it says here that I only generated $10," I said. "I see tons of patients there—2 days a week," I added. "This can't be right."

Everyone in the room just stared at me. The smell of the yellow mustard that had been put out for us to make cold cut sandwiches was stinging my nose. The buzz of the fluorescent lights annoyed me. The silence persisted.

"Where's my money!?" I demanded. I remained respectful, but I was clearly angry.

"I don't know," he responded—seeming embarrassed and annoyed. "It's complicated," he said. "You wouldn't understand...trust me."

I got a sick feeling in my stomach. Again, "Trust me." Again, he was trying to play on my empathy, but really he was trying to take advantage.

The bottom line is that there would be no bonus. No one "knew" where the money collected on my behalf was. My colleagues often complained about collections, but I didn't trust discussing this with them, particularly after my experience with the Harlem clinic. Basically, I had been working hard at the hospital, building a great reputation and practice, expecting them to handle the business side with the same standards and integrity I had on the medical side. Instead, as we used to say in the Bronx, once again, I got "played." They didn't know where the money for the services I had provided was, but all the staff members got Coach bags and an open bar at the holiday party. Thinking of Maya Angelou's quote, "When someone shows you who they are, believe them," it was time for me to face reality.

MOXIE MINDSET EXERCISES

1. People sometimes violate our trust – but it is said that we don't have to worry about trusting other people if we know we can trust ourselves to protect our own interests. Describe a time someone violated your trust but you responded in a constructive way? What did you do? Why was it helpful? How about a time you wish you had responded differently? How would you respond now?

2. I often hear doctors complain of feeling taken advantage of in a financial situation, say with respect to their incentive pay if they are employed, yet when questioned, they don't seem to know much about the details. Wouldn't we want to know how much of a medication a patient may have taken if someone came in complaining of over dosage? With respect to my pay incentive, it had never occurred to me to inquire about how well the people collecting money did their job—and how they'd be accountable to me. I've heard of doctors chasing high salaries, but signing contracts that required that they turn over any outside income to their employers, or being subject to unacceptable restrictive covenants. We have to remember to take the time to understand the details of the agreements we make. Remember, "The devil is in the details!" Describe a time you wished you had thought more about the details of an agreement you made. What more should you have considered?

CHAPTER 6

······························

What Really Matters Is Whether You Can Trust You

I was disheartened to think that my boss, the staff, the hospital, and the system that I had worked so hard to serve would betray me. My friends who had their own practices said that collections are really straight forward, so if they were not, something was awry. I had accepted a role in which I provided a service and trusted them with the business part. If I couldn't trust them to also look out for my interests, then I didn't see how continuing there was going to work.

As I considered my options, I was disturbed to hear similar complaints from colleagues in other hospitals. And to add insult to injury, we, doctors, people who were generally regarded among the smartest, were being told that we were not capable, or should not concern ourselves, with the business side and the money aspect of medicine. This was all while being held accountable for bringing in money and making decisions that affected people's lives. I felt great frustration. I went to great schools. I had great credentials. I did great work. Why was I experiencing this resistance to getting paid fairly in a reasonable work environment? I was coming to realize that sometimes others would disappoint me. This could not be an excuse for me to disappoint me.

MOXIE MINDSET EXERCISE

1. In business, and life in general, we have to deal with how things are, rather than how they should be. Where are you still complaining about how something "should be" in your career, business, family, city, country or in other relationships, instead facing reality and moving toward a situation you'd prefer? Instead of focusing on whether we can trust others or circumstances, it is more constructive to think about what we must do to trust in ourselves, and find the best way to respond to the situation. Where in your life are you "sitting on the nail," rather than trusting yourself to get up and get what you want?

CHAPTER 7

....

Say Goodbye to the Sugar Daddy Mindset

I transitioned out of my employed, academic position without a particular plan. I did not want to work in another politically toxic hospital environment. I did, however, need to work. I didn't have other income, a rich spouse, or a sugar daddy. I was able to make money working part-time in various settings, including a student health center clinic and out of someone else's private practice. I was supporting myself fine, but I felt duped. I had worked so hard to build an interesting career, yet found myself in the medical gig economy. I could have easily left New York City. Anywhere else would have offered easy employment opportunities. I could easily have become a rich, big fish outside of the Big Apple. The problem was that I didn't want to go somewhere else. I wanted to be successful in New York. I had no real guarantee that I wouldn't face the same problems in other places—and I wouldn't be where I wanted to be outside of work.

I realized that if I wanted to have the kind of life that I wanted, where I wanted, I was going to have to work on myself. I was going to have to start learning about the business side of medicine, finances, operations and marketing, and master it the way I had the clinical part. I was going to have to learn some new things. I was going to have to get outside my comfort zone. I was going to have to give up my sugar daddy mindset.

As I said earlier, I didn't have a sugar daddy to pay my bills—but my initial unwillingness to take responsibility for the business aspect of my career was part of a sugar daddy mindset. In some ways, it was odd that I had developed this type of thinking. I was a very independent person, raised in the Bronx, Harlem and Brooklyn. Although I came from a very educated, middle class family, I was of that "latch-key kid" generation, having grown up in a single-parent home. We were not babied. If I wanted something, I was expected to make it happen. I went to an exclusive boarding school in Connecticut, for which I had earned a full scholarship. I graduated from Harvard College at the age of 20. Although I had little money at the time, I worked and gained sponsorships that let me travel around the world. Medical school at Yale led to a coveted training position at the University of California, San Francisco. I had climbed many mountains. And I was tired. No, I didn't want to become a kept woman, but I wanted someone else to make sure I got what I wanted, doing things my way. Adulting is hard work.

Don't get me wrong. I'm not talking about being lazy. I was willing to work, but only the part of the work that I liked to do. I wasn't willing to take responsibility for everything that needed to be done—the money part. But I wanted the money to work out. I needed the money to work out. Having a sugar daddy mindset is having the belief that someone else is responsible for personal wants and needs. It is a mindset of rigidity. It is one of attachment to what should happen without taking responsibility for what is happening.

I was sitting on the nail of not finding a work environment I wanted. Regardless of the career opportunity, it had to be someplace I wanted to be, a place in which I would have an enjoyable career, grow professionally, fulfill my purpose, and do well financially. I loved what I did. I just never expected to have to worry about how I could do this work that I loved, in an environment I loved, and get paid. It soon became obvious to me that getting off of the nail would mean starting my own practice. I wasn't finding what I wanted. I would have to create it.

MOXIE MINDSET EXERCISE

1. Part of the appeal of sugar daddy mindset is that one does not have to take responsibility. It's not that we cannot work interdependently with others—it's just ultimately our own responsibility to get our needs met. Where do you have a sugar daddy mindset in your life?

CHAPTER 8

....

Microsoft Is Not a Mom and Pop Shop

My fear of being able to master the business side of medicine aside, I was also uncertain that I even wanted to run my own practice. While some friends who were not in medicine, with whom I had discussed my ideas, thought it all sounded exciting, I was worried about getting stuck running "the corner shop." Like a perpetual bachelor, I worried about the life of a business owner being boring and feeling trapped with responsibilities. This was my mindset, until a friend pointed out, "Microsoft is not a mom and pop shop."

I realized that I had been thinking of having a business as something small, uninteresting, and burdening—as if it were an obligation. But having a business is what one makes of it. Microsoft is a business and it is not a Mom and Pop shop. It has changed people's lives all over the world. Being able to see running a business as something exciting and interesting, rather than a burden, was a big shift for me. I had spent much of my life learning medicine, but I realized that if I was going to start a business, I would have to become a student again—this time of business. It was time to learn new things. It's not that I had done anything wrong at my other jobs. The Universe was just trying to direct me toward the path that led to my next place. I had learned all that I needed to learn from those positions. The Universe was showing me that I was destined to take a different road from the one on which I began.

When I decided to get up off the nail and start my own business, things seemed to happen fast for me. I continued to work part-time at a clinic, as well as out of my friend's office. I was working independently, but we arranged to split the collections in exchange for him handling the business. He was better at collecting money than they had been at the hospital, so this seemed okay, but we had no formal agreement. As my reputation and practice grew, I realized that this arrangement was a mistake. When I tried to formalize our agreement, it became clear that we had different goals. I had, once again, drifted into the sugar daddy mindset, expecting that he would be honest and take care of things for me. I hadn't protected myself. This time, however, I got off the nail much faster. When I realized it was no longer a good idea to work out of my colleague's space, I was up and running my practice in another location in less than one month.

MOXIE MINDSET EXERCISE

1. Describe a time when a change in how you saw things instantly inspired you to take action.

_____

_____

_____

_____

_____

_____

_____

_____

_____

_____

_____

_____

_____

CHAPTER 9

....

Imperfect Action Is the Way

I can't say that I would recommend that someone start a practice the way I did. However, some people have to be pushed in the pool before they will swim. That was me. Sometimes it's the thing we were not wanting that gets us going.

I had left academia and had been working out of a colleague's office for just over a year when I realized that I had put myself in a situation similar to the one I had encountered at the hospital—and just on a hand shake. I was building a practice and a following, while letting someone with whom I had no formal contract, handle the business. At first it was one of my side hustles. But as it grew, I realized we had to formalize things. My colleague did not agree. When I realized that I was going to have to step out on my own, I had to get things up and going with military speed and efficiency. Luckily, I had been proactive in connecting with doctors across a variety of specialties, and would often go out and meet potential referring doctors, much like a pharmaceutical rep does. I was aware of many of the resources available to get myself going.

It would have been nice to have had the chance to plan some things, but starting a practice worked out well for me despite having to do it unexpectedly. It was because of my willingness to take imperfect action. It was also because I had already started working on myself despite being unsure that I would start this type of business. Imperfect action is important, especially in today's world, where circumstances are constantly changing—even with perfect planning. We often have to execute without experience or practice. If you are going to run a successful, profitable practice, get ready to change direction from time to time. In other industries, like tech, they thrive on the thought of change. Medicine is a different sort of industry, we deal with consequences more than tech companies do, but we too must learn to roll with change. Make plans when you can, but be ready for change. Remember the saying, "People make plans, and God laughs." You still have to take action. That's life on these private practice streets.

MOXIE MINDSET EXERCISE

1. Has there ever been a time in your life when you had to step up and take action before you thought you were ready? What were you afraid of? Was it as scary as you thought? How can you use what you learned from that experience to help you move forward now?

CHAPTER 10

The Spoils Go to the Coachable

I knew that it was important to control my personal overhead, and in the crazy New York City real estate market, I was able to secure a place to live that would be considered expensive anywhere else, but a steal by New York standards. Okay, it was a two bedroom apartment that cost more than a five bedroom house in Dallas—but less than a parking spot on Central Park South. But it was mine. I had even "met someone" that I had thought would be a great life partner, and we had a beautiful baby girl together. But I soon fell on another nail in the porch. I was thrilled about my baby, but not so much the man, so it was single parenthood for me.

I had this busy, independent practice that depended on me working for the money to come. I was running said business with a beautiful, yummy, new baby on my hip that I wanted to spend time with. I also needed a nanny for whom I had to find a salary. I was feeling overwhelmed and tired from the physical and mental demands of motherhood—of both the baby and business I had birthed. I was getting what I wanted but, once again, was feeling unsure of how I was going to make it all work. I wanted to work less, but my work was my primary source of income. Now, with a baby, I needed more money than I made before, but I wanted to work less.

I don't know what I would have done if I had not gone to that workshop by the late, great, Phil Laut. I saw mention of the workshop in an email. All the message said was that he would be giving a workshop at a nearby church.

A few years prior, I had read a powerful book he wrote, called *Money Is My Friend*. With the copyright being sometime in the 1970s, and the book requiring me to check multiple stores and sites to find it, I was under the impression that the author had died long ago. I don't know why I thought that—but he was alive and would be giving a workshop on our relationship with money. Not only did I attend, but I hired him as my first business coach. The cost was $3000 for 90 days of weekly calls. My friends thought I was either crazy, or stupid, until I doubled my business while working part-time.

Phil helped me see how powerful mindset is with respect to business and money. A big part of Phil's coaching involved uncovering our beliefs, in this case around money, that don't serve us, then creating affirmations that support new beliefs. When I started working with Phil, I was stuck in the loop of believing that being a single mother and spending time with my daughter, while running a successful business, was impossible. The affirmation around that was, "My business supports my family and my family supports my business." When I was feeling overwhelmed or guilty, I would use that to get my moxie back. It wasn't necessary to know why it was true. It was important to believe it. Phil helped me see the power of great coaching—even in business.

MOXIE MINDSET EXERCISE

1. When I shared with people that I was paying a coach to help me better run my business, they reacted to the cost, feeling that I was spending too much money. I thought of the cost as an investment, as it brought me so much more in value. As doctors, we sometimes deal with patients who complain about spending $20 for the value of better health. How do you feel about investing in yourself? What is the difference between an expense versus an investment?

CHAPTER 11

....

Expect Competition from Unusual Suspects

"If you think you're enlightened, go spend a week with your family."

—Ramm Das

Again, my business grew. I was starting to get media attention that I hadn't looked for. As a new mommy, I didn't feel I looked my best, and I wasn't really trying to be in front of cameras. But the Universe said it was my time to do this. Aware of the power of media attention, I used a local news clip, in which I wore a fabulous dress by Byron Lars (he used to design for Barbie Dolls), and again, my practice boomed. Now, I was challenged with space issues in the location that I was renting part-time. I didn't have access to my space even five days a week, and I had only two examination rooms. As my office space was shared, I didn't feel comfortable storing all of my business documents there, so even home was feeling a bit cluttered. I also wanted to move into a space that I controlled and had access to 24 hours a day. It took me a few years to find a space in the location I wanted. The day that what would become my own office space was identified, I was literally passing by the building in a taxi when my real estate agent called. She said the address as we were approaching the location, and it all seemed like magic. The location was perfect. Shortly after that, we saw the space—which I loved. Soon I was in contract, looking for architects and contractors to build out my dream office. The space not being move-in-ready was the only part that wasn't in order. It was expensive to build, but it was something I had to do to get off the nail of working in a space that was limiting my growth. As is usually the case in Manhattan, working with the contractors, the city and the landlord was a bit of a nightmare. Little was straightforward. There were delays. It cost more money than projected. Eventually, however, I was able to move into my new space. I did it, but by the time I was ready to boom in my new space, the economy was bust. We were in the middle of the financial crisis of 2008.

My patients were losing their jobs. People who still had jobs and insurance were afraid to leave their desks to come in no matter how itchy they were. Insurance companies were slow to pay. Financing was being pulled or not offered. Patients who did come had high deductibles that they had to be chased to pay, were looking for discounts, and became increasingly demanding. Suddenly, dermatologists were not just competing with each other, but with everybody, as an explosion of med spas offering cosmetic procedures occurred. Non-core specialists, from psychiatrists and dentists, to gynecologists and radiologists, used their licenses to purchase injectables, and got into the aesthetics market. I was starting to feel like a failure. I couldn't understand why what had seemed so basic, throwing up a shingle and starting a medical practice, had become so hard. People told me I was doing so well, but I couldn't understand how they could say that when it seemed I was about to lose everything I built.

One day, while looking at the website analytics for my business and comparing them to those of some other dermatologists, I noticed that our websites were ranked similarly. However, I was surprised to find that one outlier website was getting three times the traffic for a particular dermatologic term than dermatologists were. It was the website of a med spa owned by...an eye doctor. And it wasn't the spa of just any eye doctor. It was an eye doctor who was sending me the COMPLICATIONS from his office for the skin treatments that he was doing for cash. His website came up frequently when searching dermatologic terms. I found this fascinating. Here I was, having graduated from Harvard and Yale, a board certified dermatologist, trained in one of the most competitive programs in the world. I had been on television. I was known. I seemed to have done everything right—yet people were going to an eye doctor's website more frequently than mine when looking for acne treatment. I had an Ivy League education and years of experience, but people turned over hundreds of dollars to the newly high-school-graduated sales rep at the cosmetic store before they came to see me—often complaining about paying their $20 co-pay.

Despite all I had done, it seemed that the general public didn't know, or didn't understand the difference between what I offered, and what an eye doctor offered, with respect to skin health. It was at this moment I realized that although I had grown my business, I still needed to work on my business skills. Things had been easy when I started this journey. When I started, payments and credit were flowing. When I started, there wasn't constant disruption. I would not only have to compete with my dermatologist peers. I would have to compete with other people who were pretending to be "dermatologists." The barbarians were at the gates of small business dermatology. I was going to have to get up off the nail, once again. I wasn't lying down this time. I hadn't noticed, however, that someone had used an unusually long nail on the porch floor and it had, figuratively of course, slipped out of place, and into my side. I was going to have to, once again, kick up my business game.

MOXIE MINDSET EXERCISE

1. It is in the more challenging times, not the easy ones, that we determine how well we've mastered something. Describe a challenging time that led you toward an accomplishment?

_____

_____

_____

_____

_____

_____

_____

_____

CHAPTER 12

....

Being "A Boss" and Being "The Boss" Are Not the Same

"Freedom is what you do with what's been done to you."

—Jean-Paul Sartre

Once, my daughter, who was about 9-years-old at the time, advised me that I didn't have to go to work, and that I could do whatever I wanted to do, because I was "the boss." She had only ever known me as a business owner. Her perception of what it meant to run your own business, however age appropriate, made me laugh. How cute to see life so simply.

Most people are familiar with life as employee rather than as a boss, simply because more people are employees than bosses. We grow up with the idea that "boss" is this coveted, God-like position, in which we are free and all powerful. We think being the boss means we can do whatever we want. This explains why it is popular now for new college graduates to immediately aspire to start their own businesses, because they are too "cool" to work for somebody else. Everybody wants to be "a boss."

Yes, when you are the boss, you have freedom and power—such as you get to decide the maternity leave policy. A boss may take all the maternity leave she wants. But all the bills usually come in the boss's name. If the boss runs a small private doctor's office, and the boss also sees the patients, there may not be a business left after the boss comes back from the three-year maternity leave she took because that's what she wanted to do, and she is the boss. Even if the boss has outside money to keep the practice going despite her not being there, the patients have needs, and will likely look elsewhere to have them met. Yes, a boss has freedom, but freedom has consequences. When you are a business owner, or "the boss," you are never entirely free the way many people think.

Further, when you start an independent physician's practice, remember, unless the business has some other source of income (leveraged or passive) which provides you with income enough to live on when you are not working, you still, in a sense, have a job. You just own the job, as Robert Kiyosaki, author of *Rich Dad Poor Dad*, says. Even when you are a business owner who doesn't have to be there, or an investor, who is simply letting the money do the work, it's still important to continue to be conscious of what is going on with your business.

Being the boss does have great rewards. But sometimes, being an employee is much easier. Luckily, New York City has some great resources for aspiring small business owners, to help them make that transition. One is a free-to-low-cost workshop that has been offered for decades, that trains people to set up all kinds of businesses—from hot dog vendors, to doctors and lawyers. Over the years, I've referred many friends and acquaintances to the program when they've asked me for advice about business. Some eventually started successful businesses. Others found the program helpful—but did not start businesses. When they saw all that was involved in being the boss, they wanted to stay employees.

In one of my favorite books, *The 48 Rules of Power*, an entertaining and instructive manual about dealing with power dynamics, the first rule is "Never outshine the master, unless the master is on the way down." What's the significance? We may think of "the boss" as a position of power, which it is. But it is also a position of insecurity. Others depend on you. Others want things from you, and they compete with you. Others hold you responsible, sometimes unfairly. People often don't understand *your* struggles. We complain when our boss is insecure. Only when we become the boss, do we realize *why* our boss was insecure.

In an animal behavior class that I took in college, we watched a documentary about a species of red deer in which the males competed to be the alpha male, the dominant male, who had the best access to reproduce with females during mating season. This is called agonistic rank, or dominance hierarchy. Although it is a privilege to be the alpha male, the stud of the bunch, once that status is achieved, the male's life expectancy is much shorter. The alpha male gets to have more babies, but he also has to constantly fight off other males who want his high rank in the group. If he isn't killed or knocked from his position, all of the competition eventually wears him out and he soon dies.

I am sure that it was, in part, my fears about the challenges of being in charge that made me hesitate to start my own practice. The thought of taking on these challenges was scary. Yes, there were benefits like freedom, tax breaks, and the potential to make more money. But there was always the risk of failure and increased responsibility.

To endure both the fears and realities of becoming a boss, you have to make sure that you are mentally, physically, and socially strong enough to survive the demands and changes of being the chief. Even when you have a team of people to delegate responsibilities to, when you are the business owner, especially in medicine, you can't completely tune out like you can when you are an employee. Get clear as to whether or not you can handle the challenges of running your own practice. They *will* come.

MOXIE MINDSET EXERCISE

1. List 10 benefits of being your own boss, and 10 things you think will be harder. Come up with strategies to address the harder things.

_____

_____

_____

_____

_____

_____

_____

_____

_____

_____

CHAPTER 13

....

Business Owner vs. Employee Mindset

Business is a game of psychological and spiritual mindset. If one is to build and run a profitable private practice, it is important to get comfortable with receiving and managing money. Money is not just about bookkeeping, accounting, and financing. Money is not just paper and coins. It's a belief about the value and flow of resources. Money is a highly emotional subject. One might think that everyone has a positive attitude toward receiving money, but is that true? Doctors often see money as being at odds with caring about patients—yet they complain about not having enough money. In order to have a profitable medical practice, it is necessary to work on one's money mindset. With the wrong mindset, payments won't get collected, employees won't be held accountable, and new services won't be explored. Business coaching can feel more like therapy than financial planning.

Like it or not, a private practice is a business. Business owners need a different mindset than employees do. What the leader believes and feels directly affects what happens, including the positive or negative flow of money in the business. Unless you were raised in a family of business owners, and I would add, successful and happy business owners, you are probably more familiar with the employee mindset that with the boss mindset. What's the difference?

Salaried employees generally make an agreement upfront and can expect payment every two weeks. Their mindset when they are negotiating this salary determines how much money flows to them (we've all heard about how women undervalue themselves). After the salary has been negotiated, however, an employee's mindset and feelings going forward (unless they don't do their work, get fired, or are on commission) does not directly affect their income.

The business owner's mindset, on the other hand, constantly impacts the flow of money. The business owner is constantly making decisions, negotiating, and executing activities that directly affect the bottom line. The owner has to manage employees, clients and vendors. What the owner believes and feels about receiving and accumulating money will affect all aspects of the business.

I was surprised to find out that I was actually sabotaging myself and my patients with my money mindset in my reluctance to offer a particular service to patients on a self-pay basis. Like most doctors in America, even most dermatologists, I have always participated in health insurance plans. When I started out in private practice, cosmetic services were becoming more and more popular. Many of my peers were excited about this as a means of income that they could control. As I listened to people talk about certain procedures, their focus seemed to be on money, not patient care. I didn't like their energy. This made me reluctant to do cosmetic services. Non-dermatologists, even non-physicians, with little training were also starting to offer some of these services, mostly motivated by money. As one would expect, more and more we began hearing about, and seeing patients who had experienced complications from procedures done by inexperienced practitioners.

One day, a patient came into my practice who had a complication from a procedure she had at a spa. This procedure was one that I did, but I didn't advertise it much. When I did do it, it was for a medical reason that, as far as I knew, only one insurance plan covered. I asked why she would go to a spa to have a procedure done. Didn't she know that they were likely not as well trained? Her response humbled me and changed my mindset.

"Do you do this procedure?" she asked.

"Yes," I said.

"Are you well trained at doing it?" she continued.

"Yes," I said, "I do it well, but I want to focus on the medical side."

She wasn't impressed at all.

She continued, "Well, if you know how to do the procedure well, but you won't do it for me, where then shall I go?"

Drop the mic.

Although that patient had come to me for treatment, I should have sent her a payment for a valuable business coaching session. She showed me that what was really influencing my decisions was my fear of discussing money and egoic concerns about what other people would think of me if I added cosmetic services and made more money. Until then, I had convinced myself that I set things up the way they were, purely because I cared so much about other people. But other people wanted me to provide this service. Other people were put in danger by having to seek it elsewhere. And despite it being an opportunity for me to make more money, something I claimed I wanted, I resisted adding this service. When I realized that it was my mindset, and that this opportunity for me to make more money was "for the good of all concerned," I made some changes.

Even when accepting payment via health insurance plans, mindset is an issue. When I provided services covered by insurance, I didn't have to take responsibility for the price. However, I had to make sure that we collected the money from the insurance company. In the days before high deductible plans this was easier. After appointments, we'd send in a bill and would be paid for our services. As long as I didn't have an issue about sending in the bill, neither I, nor the patients, had to address our money mindsets. When insurance began to more commonly involve dealing with copays and deductibles, and we had to bill the patients in addition to the insurance companies, this is when we also had to deal with how our *patients* felt about money. When you have a business, you deal not only with your money mindset, you must also manage that of others--patients, vendors, employees, etc. When an employee has the responsibility to collect money for the business, their mindset around money will impact cash flow. The business owner has to have worked on his or her own mindset in order to coach employees on how to handle theirs.

I've had staff members who were uncomfortable collecting co-payments from patients who resisted paying at the time of their visit. They would let these patients in to be seen despite our policy that they pay before their appointments. By the way, these were small amounts of money. The patients refusing to follow policy were not even people claiming financial distress. They were simply disrespectful. In situations such as this, doctors could be draconian and simply fire staff members for failing to follow office policy. Having had to make this mindset journey myself, I realized that with a little coaching, however, I would be able to retain some excellent employees who, like me, needed a little change in perspective.

"That money you didn't collect is your money," I pointed out once to a receptionist.

"He didn't want to pay right now," she explained. "He said he'd pay us next week." I imagined someone trying that tactic in a restaurant. They'd be confronted by the police.

"Okay," I said. "Since that is where your money comes from, I guess I'll have to hold payroll until next week."

She worked for me for years and we never had that conversation again.

I run my practice with the understanding that no patient comes to see me because I have bills. I get money in exchange for bringing some value they are seeking. The emphasis is my patients' needs. I am now of the mindset that I can feel good about getting paid to meet them. My business has needs that I alone cannot fulfill. This creates job opportunities for other people, as well as other businesses. When I look at it like that, I am earning, receiving, and accumulating money for the good of all concerned. That makes me feel good! Hands clapping! Yay!

One of the most impactful money mindset shifts I had was after a conversation with my first business coach, Phil, about pricing. He taught me a lesson about the arrogance of doctors—though it wasn't the one I might have expected. I wanted to help people and make more money, but my mindset was in the way. I was talking about a procedure I did differently than plastic surgeons, but charged less.

"What is different about the way you do it?" my coached asked.

"Instead of making a big incision, I take the lesion out in pieces through a small one. It's simple. I don't charge much for it, and the patient has a much smaller scar," I bragged.

"Patients pay the plastic surgeon's fees?" he asked.

"Yes," I said. I was feeling righteous with respect to the doctors in plastics.

"If you do it in a simpler way, with a smaller scar, you should charge more, he said.

I didn't understand.

"But…" I started to respond.

"Listen," he said. "Stop thinking you are better than your patients by charging them too little."

"What?" I asked in disbelief. Had he just suggested that it was arrogant to charge a lower price?

He continued, "Don't think you're better than people," he said. "Your patients could have done what you did—you aren't better than they are." We were not using a video phone application, so he couldn't see my eyes get big and my jaw drop as he spoke.

"They could've gone to college like you did—right?"

Although I have always thought of myself as a person who empowers patients, when I stripped away how I wanted to appear, I realized that I had bought into that patronizing mindset of the powerful doctor and the vulnerable patient. Just because someone had come seeking services in my area of expertise, did not mean that they didn't also have agency. Patients already had power. They didn't need me to give it to them. Didn't I also enjoy the services of other people who learned something I did not? Didn't I pay them? Why did I think that people who came to access what I happened to learn could not pay?

My first impulse was to say that it wasn't true that everyone could have gone to college. The world isn't fair. Not everyone had the same opportunities and aptitude. But when I thought about it, people overcome obstacles all the time. How many books have been written by highly successful people telling their stories of having overcome obstacles? It did seem like arrogance to speak limitation onto other people's lives. To my surprise, I found myself agreeing.

"They could have gone to medical school, trained, passed the boards, and gotten the experience that you have after years of practice, to know what you know, to solve the problem for themselves—right?" he continued.

Again, I had to agree. No, becoming a board certified dermatologist is not easy—but I did it. Who am I to say that someone else couldn't do it too? Now, not only did disagreeing seem incorrect—it seemed patronizing.

"Whatever you charge," he finished, "it would be hard to charge too much. In fact, it's likely an incredible discount given the time and money you invested in learning to solve those problems."

Drop the mic.

Many of us in medicine think we are being "good" by being martyrs and enablers. We think we are helping other people, and in order to do that, we shouldn't have our own needs met. And then we complain. Could it be, however, that what is really happening is that we are not acting in the interest of others, but really looking to feel needed and important? Do we, perhaps, have low self-esteem and give too much so that we feel valuable and needed? We burn ourselves out pretending we are helping, when what we are doing is disempowering patients so that we get to play the hero. And when we burnout, or our practices are not financially viable, who then can be helped by our medical services?

On the other hand, undervaluing my services as a doctor was also being a punk. The culture of medicine grooms doctors to undervalue themselves. Our training involves sacrificing our youth and serving with little pay for years as the price of admission. The dynamic of health insurance, the most common way people now pay for care, involves a third party, someone else telling us what our services were worth. With the culture of malpractice litigation, others make more than we do off of perceived mistakes, than we are rewarded for great outcomes like saving a life. And now we are fighting off an onslaught of extenders who don't want to invest the time to train, but want to rush right out into practice and compete with doctors, hiding behind the doctor's license. So, I realized that charging too little was also disrespectful to myself.

With this shift in my mindset, I felt so much lighter and empowered in implementing services in my business that involved pricing that I controlled. It also reduced my anxiety around discussing money with patients and people that I paid. My coach wasn't saying that my goal should be to have the highest price in the market. Pricing comes down to the perfect storm of how much money someone requires for a service, and what the client it is willing to pay in order to receive it. It's all spiritual. Pricing should work for "the good of all concerned."

I've worked with people who charged more and gave poor service because their intention was bad faith—to take value but not give. I've also had vendors who charged too little, and ended up giving poor service and feeling resentful because their needs were not being met. The right price isn't the highest or the lowest price. The right price is the one that makes the seller feel good about providing the service, and makes the buyer feel good about receiving it.

Many doctors have a hard time building a profitable practice because they haven't dealt with their negative mindset around money. The bottom line is that for a practice to run and heal the patients it serves, payments must occur. Our fears and feelings about money, not just our technical knowledge about financial matters, can be just as important to our success or failure. It's important to feel good about receiving money for your services as a doctor. It's important to feel worthy of receiving.

Doctors often see giving attention to money as being at odds with caring about patients, which is their purpose for being in medicine. They neglect attention to money matters with comments like, "I'm not in medicine for the money." Yet, we hear doctors complaining about not being paid enough by insurance companies to cover their costs and spend enough time with their patients. We hear doctors complaining about not having enough money to pay their student loan bills. The epidemic of "doctor burnout" is tied to issues around the economics of medicine. Many doctors who aspired to heal, end up leaving medicine all together, resulting in a physician shortage, and patients being underserved in many communities.

Doctors sometimes say they don't care about money, yet it was money that allowed the doctor to go to medical school. Even if the money wasn't the doctor's own, but someone else's (parents, trust fund, lenders, scholarship, etc.), wasn't it money that provided the opportunity? Saying you don't care about the money may sound cute on your medical school application essay, but it's an immature mindset. It will hurt you if you are running a business. Even if you are volunteering as a doctor, money provides you the time and resources to serve. A boss who has the responsibility to make sure that everything runs has to have a mature mindset toward money. Even non-profit organizations have to be run like businesses because although the income and resources are often donated, they still need these resources to operate. A boss who needs an income and wants a profit needs to have a positive mindset toward money because their mindset is the one that affects the flow of money into the business.

The bottom line is that money is a tool we use in the world to do most things. It is a flow of energy and resources. Money is neither good nor bad—it just is. It's our feelings and beliefs about money that determine how it flows to us. And, really, if you didn't go into medicine for the money, and you care about patients, you owe it to them, and to yourself, to learn about money so that you can continue to serve.

MOXIE MINDSET EXERCISE

1. In order to run a profitable business, you have to get comfortable with the subject of money—be it money going in or out. Money isn't really about money itself. It's about what money represents. It's a mindset issue tied to feelings about survival, self-esteem, and love. What does having more than enough money feel like to you? What does not having enough money feel like? How do you feel when you are around people who have much more money, or much less money, than you do? Profit starts with feeling good about receiving and accumulating money. Then you can make decisions in support of that feeling.

CHAPTER 14

....

Beware the "Doctor Drop"

Even as we complain that our profession is losing respect, being a doctor still is associated with certain esteem, privilege and resources. This can attract kindness, access, and respect, or it can attract people who want to use or take advantage of the doctor. When the usual laws of courtesy, reciprocity, and fairness are on hold because one of the parties is a physician, I call this the "doctor drop." Some people believe that just because they are dealing with a doctor, easy money and favors, should drop into their laps. They should get to raid your wallet and use your reputation to their benefit. It's a special tax for being a doctor. The "doctor drop" can turn relationships sour, kill a profitable practice, and cause burnout in a New York minute.

Some people who are focused only on the most lucrative services and the fact that it is primarily an outpatient specialty, view dermatology as a field in which people are paid easy money, money that they don't deserve, to provide services that are not important. Dermatologists fall victim to the "doctor drop" more often than doctors in other specialties. These people usually fixate on the highest ticket service in dermatology, assuming that is what we do all day. To them, all dermatologists are "Botox slingers." We aren't treating itchy babies, genital warts, perianal abscesses, blistering skin diseases or shingles. If they can't get an appointment soon enough, it's because we don't care about them or are getting our nails done, not booked out. By creating a narrative that we somehow don't deserve and didn't earn whatever we have, it makes it easier to justify taking advantage of us.

An experience with an online marketing company, for which I did some beta testing, revealed to me the dangerous spirit of the "doctor drop." When I opened my own office during the financial crisis in 2008, a member of my staff came across an opportunity to try out a new platform that allowed patients to make appointments online. The company wanted to work with dentists, plastic surgeons and dermatologists only. I didn't understand why the specialty mattered, but I didn't think about it too much. It was free and didn't require any additional effort on my part, other than setting up the profile. I gave it a go.

As we participated in this beta testing, I was very impressed with the results. Many new patients found us using this platform. It was nice that their appointments were already made by the time we were contacted. I liked the types of people that the platform brought to my office. After a year or so, the company contacted me for feedback. They wanted to know if I would be willing to pay, at some future time, for this service. It was clearly bringing me value. I told them it was something I would be willing to pay for.

Using the practices of the doctors and dentists in the beta testing as examples, the company was able to showcase their start-up to much acclaim. Over the next year, I saw the company grow in the news. The founder was all over the local and national media as a darling in "healthcare" innovation. One of the richest companies in the world started investing. The start-up was soon valued at tens of millions of dollars, and the founder was an overnight millionaire. Not only were they successful, they were celebrated as a humane and great place to work, offering their employees all kinds of benefits like great health insurance, catered organic lunches, yoga, and other wellness services.

The following year I was contacted by the company and informed that they were going to begin charging for the service. They told me the price, and I was happy to pay, as the platform had been bringing business. The next year, a sales representative from the company called to get feedback and renew my subscription.

"It has been great," I said. "Of course, I want to continue."

"Great," the sales representative replied. "So let's get started. What's your specialty?"

I have to admit, I was a little hurt by the question. It might have been a bit of an ego issue. I had been using the platform for years; I was one of the earliest users. The staff had come to my office to get feedback and brainstorm several times. It was a local company. I thought we had a relationship. But ego aside, I didn't understand why my specialty was important to renew my subscription.

"My specialty?" I asked. "Why does that matter?" There was silence on the line. As I waited for an answer, a thought came to me.

"Are you charging me more because I'm a dermatologist?" I asked. Again, silence. But this time it was short.

"Yes we are," responded the voice on the other line. "And we can!" he added with emphasis.

I was stunned. This company had built their business showcasing the practices of dermatologists, which had allowed them success beyond anything a practicing doctor could imagine. Yes, we had gotten to use it free for a while, but we didn't get stock options for our service. They needed our cooperation to build their business. They needed to use what we had already invested in *our* practices. And they raised fast money standing in the virtuous stardust of "healthcare" when really they were a digital marketing company. Their employees enjoyed greater benefits than anyone who works in healthcare. Yet, they felt it was acceptable to charge certain doctors, the doctors whose shoulders they were standing on, more to provide the same service—rationalizing that we had too much. The way I saw it, would the staff at his office pay $20 for the same cup of coffee at the coffee cart that others purchased for $1—because their founder was on Bloomberg?

"Wow!" I responded, giving myself a moment to think. Luckily, I already knew that my practice was not dependent on someone else. I had benefited by using the platform, but I had a booming practice before they came along. They were not the source of my good.

"Well I don't like that," I shared.

"Well, we can do it," insisted the sales representative.

"Yes, you can do it," I said. "and I can NOT renew my subscription, although I valued your service. I can also be sure to tell all my colleagues that you are charging us more for the same service."

"Hold on, ma'am," the sales representative said.

He put me on hold. A few minutes later he came back conceding that perhaps I was right that dermatologists shouldn't pay more (they had been charging us TRIPLE for the same services). OUCH! I got a "courtesy" discount that year, in "appreciation" of my years of support. More importantly, they stopped the "dermatologist drop" and started charging everyone the same price.

The "doctor drop" isn't always directly about money. It's sometimes about trying to hold the doctor hostage to someone else's unreasonable expectations. Years ago there was an article in The New York Times, ironically written by a doctor, suggesting that doctors should not be allowed to work part-time. The rationale was that doctors, in particular, were indebted to society, because the schools and hospitals at which they trained had been supported with government money. But isn't that also true for software engineers, lawyers, business school graduates and history professors? When does the doctor's debt end? Can we be surprised that there is a shortage of doctors and an epidemic of "burnout" if we treat the profession as indentured servitude?

Doctors are used to being held accountable for their responsibilities. Do you not hold the people in your life accountable for theirs? Patients, employers, employees, vendors, friends and family can sometimes drop their responsibilities, clinical or not, on the doctor in their lives, when they are supposed to be coming through for the doctor. It may be obligations dropping on you, the doctor, that wouldn't otherwise be appropriate, or support dropping out from under you. The treatment wouldn't be acceptable to do but for that fact that you are a doctor. If you often feel like you are having to play everyone else's position—watch out—it may be a shortcut to physician burnout, also known as the "doctor drop."

MOXIE MINDSET EXERCISES

1. Giving too much or letting someone take advantage of us may seem to the ego like generosity or kindness—but it is a violation of the law of reciprocity. Consider that it's a symptom of low self-esteem. Even what we sometimes describe as arrogance is low self-esteem. It's a need to be the hero, or the smartest or most successful person in the room. It may also be a symptom of not feeling worthy of receiving. Is there some relationship or situation in your business or personal life that feels like it is draining you or burning you out? Would you allow this if you were not a doctor? Is there something to which you need to say no? Why have you been allowing it? Do you feel uncomfortable receiving? What specific action can you take to make things feel right?

CHAPTER 15

....

Don't Over Cherish Humility—Market

"Don't be so humble. You're not that great."

—Golda Meir

When I was growing up, outside of the Yellow Pages (for those of you too young to remember, that was a paper phone directory), it was illegal in New York State, for doctors to advertise. Pharmaceutical companies were not allowed to advertise either. Marketing and advertising were regarded as a type of deception. The perception was that good doctors didn't need to advertise. If a doctor was good, people would hear about that doctor by word-of-mouth. As for medications, the belief was that doctors should recommend what was in the best interest of the patient, selecting medications based on outcomes rather than advertisements.

Since then, the world has changed—a lot. Not only are doctors and drug companies allowed to market and advertise, marketing companies are gaining influence in all sectors of society—including healthcare. In a noisy, crowded environment like New York City, marketing is everything—even in medicine. I learned this after the recession. Until then, most of my marketing had been low budget, bootstrap, reputation-based marketing. I was in the hospital and insurance directories. I socialized and passed out my business cards. I had unique skills as a board certified dermatologist. I saw the opportunity of having a practice website early in the game, so patients were finding me online before digital marketing was an industry. People were attracted to the fact that I had gone to schools with great brands—Harvard and Yale. And ultimately, people liked what I did for them—so they told others. The patients came. I never really thought of all of this as marketing—but it was. Marketing is simply making sure people know what you can do for them.

If marketing in medicine were frowned upon in the pre-digital age, the world was in for a change with the advent of online marketing. Digital marketing would disrupt what influenced how people made decisions, even about where to get help for a medical problem, in ways we could have never predicted. Marketing, for better or worse, has become the fabric of so much of what we do. Isn't the internet driven by the advertising and marketing value?

Doctors who are reluctant to market often find themselves complaining about the person who is not a doctor, driven by a different set of ethics, who invests in marketing to persuade patients to use their services instead. Remember the eye doctor who used to send me the complications from his skin treatments? The patients had found him first. No matter how qualified we may be, we are not so great that someone who is more influential can't take business from us. If we feel we have something of value to offer, isn't it unethical for doctors not to market?

MOXIE MINDSET EXERCISE

1. How do you feel about marketing as a doctor?

_____

_____

_____

_____

_____

_____

_____

_____

_____

_____

_____

_____

_____

CHAPTER 16

·····························

Shine Bright like a Diamond

> *"We ask ourselves, 'Who am I to be brilliant, gorgeous, talented, fabulous?' Actually, who are you not to be? You are a child of God. Your playing small does not serve the world."*
>
> **—Marianne Williamson**

One afternoon during the recession, one of my favorite pharmaceutical reps came by the office. He was looking at the minimalist décor of the waiting room. I prided myself on being clean and simple. As he glanced at the walls he advised, "You might want to hire a PR agency to get yourself into some magazines."

I was confused. "I've been in many magazines," I said.

Now he was confused. "Where are they?" he asked. "Other doctors put those out all over the place."

My many magazine citations and media clips were neatly tucked away in a file cabinet. In my mind, it was cool to have been in a magazine, but I didn't really think patients would care about whether I had been. I had great qualifications and experience. Shouldn't that be good enough? I believed that if I took really good care of them, they'd know I was a great doctor and that the word would spread. Although that strategy had been working initially, in the newly more competitive world, where even physician assistants had publicists and were marketing themselves as "board certified," I didn't have an advantage hiding in the shadows. In fact, I had to admit that I had been a little afraid of seeming arrogant by filling my office with magazine covers.

After thinking about it, my assistant and I pulled out all my media and planned to spend a Saturday decorating the office with my press. Once I pulled everything out, even I was amazed at all I had done—and had taken for granted. We purchased all the plexiglass frames in the area, and had to go to the internet to find more. It was impressive, however, I was concerned about how my patients would react on Monday. When the door to the office opened, the first thing that they would see would be our new "wall of fame." I worried that patients might not trust me if I were flashing my press.

On Monday it felt like I had a completely different patient population. Patients, new and old, were so much more respectful. I was the same doctor I had been on Friday, however, it seemed that they took my advice with less resistance. I would peek out into the waiting room and literally see people grinning. Some even took pictures of the magazine covers in the waiting room. I asked my receptionists if they had noticed a difference. They said that when people walked in, they paused to look at the wall. "By the time they come up to the front desk," one of my staff said, "they have an expression on their faces that says 'I've come to the right place.'"

When you have a private practice, or any business, you don't want to be the best kept secret in town. Although I had a healthy following of patients, there were now what seemed like armies of people competing in the dermatology space. I had a great brand, but I was hiding it, in the biblical sense, under a basket. But with new media, even high school students were marketing themselves as skin care experts from their bedrooms. It was no longer always obvious to people what my qualifications meant.

Your business brand is essentially your business's reputation. It's what people say and think about your business when you are not around. The importance of branding grew as the marketplace became globalized, giving people increased options as to how to solve a problem, even a health-related one. The growing, unregulated cottage-industry of online review sites, that use the brands of other people's businesses, including doctors' offices, to drive traffic to their advertising and data collection websites, is a threat to those who neglect their reputations. Sometimes misrepresenting themselves as "customer service" or "quality of care" services, these entities do not care if the information published about your practice is true or false. These are self-interested marketing companies that will use your brand as collateral damage to enrich their shareholders. If you don't tend to your own business brand, there are many brands with no other business than to hold your brand hostage for their profit.

MOXIE MINDSET EXERCISE

1. What is your brand as a doctor? Create a brand description of the services you provide.

    _____

    _____

    _____

    _____

    _____

2. What three things can you do now to promote your brand as a doctor?

    _____

    _____

    _____

    _____

    _____

3. What is exciting about being successful? What is scary about being successful?

CHAPTER 17

....

Beware the Cuckoo Birds, Lest You Become a Dodo Bird

When you are a doctor, and you have built a thriving practice, you are in command of an incredibly valuable resource. In addition to the patients that you serve, many, many people benefit from what you have and what you do. Doctors sometimes undervalue what they are bringing to a relationship, and what it costs them, which contributes to doctor burnout and unhappiness. In order to build a profitable practice that you love and that thrives long-term, it is important to understand your own value. Be a good steward of your resources and protect your nest from cuckoo birds.

A cuckoo bird is a species of parasitic bird. It doesn't have a nest or take care of its own children. A cuckoo bird lays its eggs in the nests of other birds for them to raise its young. But it doesn't stop there. Cuckoo chicks are programed to hatch faster than the babies of the host bird species. It starts demanding food from the host parents. Think of the noisy cuckoo clock, crazily chirping to get your attention. Keeping the host parents busy providing food, the cuckoo grows quickly. Soon the cuckoo chick is strong and can push the host parents' eggs out of the nest, killing their babies—their legacy—so that the adult birds can put all of their attention on only them. Doesn't this relationship remind you of what is happening in the profession of medicine today? In case you don't get my analogy, let me spell it out for you:

Nest = your office

Eggs = your patients time, your time, your money, your attention

Host = you (the doctor)

Cuckoo bird = anyone or anything that drains your energy, attention, money, resources (i.e. pushes your eggs out of the nest).

- ▶ Inefficient technology mandated to help with data collection for other people's projects

- ▶ Insurance companies that operate in bad faith

▶ Government policies that dump responsibilities on doctors without compensation.

▶ Vendors that charge doctors more for bad service

▶ Employees who don't engage with their jobs and waste the practice's resources because they think of it as "the doctor's money," as they don't understand that they, too, get their resources from the practice

▶ Hospital administrators who get bonuses that doctors don't get, off the doctors' work

▶ Patients who threaten to write negative reviews unless the doctor works for free or commits insurance fraud and waives their deductible

Cuckoo birds are takers. Many doctors, attached to the identity of themselves as givers, or martyrs, think that they can have a practice without being mindful of what is being taken from them. Sometimes it's because they don't understand the costs and liabilities of what they do. Sometimes it's because they are afraid of standing up for themselves. But even the most generous person will burnout if they habitually violate the law of reciprocity—the law of give and take. It's not that we will always receive from the same person or place to which we gave. Sometimes we just need to think about how our own resources are being used and whether it is serving our mission and purpose.

If you find yourself dealing with cuckoos in your life or business, you need to take action. But don't feel bad. Cuckoo birds don't prey on homeless, broke birds. They look for birds that are responsible and have resources. They look for birds that have energy and pep, who can feed their greedy little hijackers.

How do we protect ourselves from medical practice cuckoos that try to drive us cuckoo, burn us out, and endanger our resources? First, we have to have a mindset of appreciation of the value that we're bringing—as well as our liabilities. We have to consider whether or not the situation serves our mission or purpose. We also have to take authority, as doctors and citizens, outside of the exam room. This may be instituting a "no show" fee in your office, firing your bookkeeper, or writing to your senator. Sometimes you have to tap into your own moxie for your benefit, rather than just being a source for others.

MOXIE MINDSET EXERCISE

1. What "cuckoo birds" are dealing with in your practice? Develop a strategy to get them out of the nest or to manage them.

CHAPTER 18

....

Moxie MD—That's Just How I Roll

I remember the day that one of the older drug reps came into my office and said, "Congratulations." I was confused. "You did it, kid," he said in that old school way. "You built a practice from fumes. You showed up in town and you didn't know anyone. You've been through it, and you're still here."

Until then, I never realized that starting a practice was a really big deal, and that despite things not being exactly as I wanted them to be, I had done something that other people regarded as an accomplishment. I was a New York City dermatologist who was running her own practice. That took a lot of moxie. Perhaps it's a good thing that I didn't know how tall the mountain and precarious the climb would be. Perhaps if I had I thought about it too much I would have never attempted the climb. I don't know how close I am to the top of my mountain, but I know I have learned a lot. Now it's time for me to share some of what I learned with other doctors who want to climb the private practice mountain, and take great care of their patients, in a profitable practice that they love. It's time to share with other doctors who want to serve, and live happy and free.

ABOUT THE AUTHOR

Dr. Dina Strachan is a board certified dermatologist, a graduate of Harvard College and Yale Medical School, and the owner of a successful dermatology practice in New York City. In addition to raising her daughter, Marley, Dr. Dina spends her time outside the clinic as a volunteer at Bellevue Hospital in Manhattan. Wearing many hats as a clinician, business owner, media personality, speaker, author and consultant, Dr. Dina strives to help doctors build and run successful independent practices by empowering them with business savvy, creativity and resources. Her mission is to serve, educate and entertain diverse audiences across a variety of industries.

Learn more at www.drdinamd.com

CREATING DISTINCTIVE BOOKS
WITH INTENTIONAL RESULTS

We're a collaborative group of creative masterminds with a mission to produce high-quality books to position you for monumental success in the marketplace.

Our professional team of writers, editors, designers, and marketing strategists work closely together to ensure that every detail of your book is a clear representation of the message in your writing.

Want to know more?
Write to us at info@publishyourgift.com
or call (888) 949-6228

Discover great books, exclusive offers, and more at
www.PublishYourGift.com

Connect with us on social media

@publishyourgift

CPSIA information can be obtained
at www.ICGtesting.com
Printed in the USA
LVHW03s2036300718
585387LV00029B/722/P